Fabulously Gluten-Free

Baked Treats and Vegetarian Cookbook

All Rights Reserved. No part of this publication may be reproduced in any form or by any means, including scanning, photocopying, or otherwise without prior written permission of the copyright holder. Copyright © 2014

Introduction

Eating gluten-free can sometimes be challenging. We find ourselves missing the taste of chocolate cake or the convenience of freshly-baked muffins. Store-bought gluten-free replacements are often dry and crumbly, not to mention usually less than tasty. Luckily, alternative flours allow for yummy homemade baked goods that satisfy a sweet tooth without the gluten. Whether you're looking for classic or bold flavors, this cookbook contains 30 naturally gluten-free recipes for fantastic baked treats. They're so good that you won't even have to tell everyone that they're gluten-free!

Table of Contents

Strawberry Toaster Pastry

Gluten-Free Cocoa Zucchini Muffin

Vanilla Bean Shortbread Cookies

Cranberry Pistachio Biscotti

Gluten-Free Cherry Pie

Berry Cobbler

Vanilla Peach Cake

Lemon Bundt Cake

Chocolate Zucchini Cake

Ginger Spice Cookies

Orange Cranberry Muffins

Milano Cookie Sandwiches

Cocoa Spice Pinwheel Cookies

Key Lime Coconut Bars

Coconut Baked Donut

Soft Pumpkin Cookies

Asian Orange Muffins

- Coconut Crisps
- Pecan Chess Pies
- Mixed Berry Trifle
- Sugar Cookies
- Apple Dump Muffins
- Fruit And Nut Cake
- Honey Nut Bun
- Orange Anzac Biscuits
- Sweet Cherry Fig Newtons
- Pineapple Upside Down Cake
- Simple Chinese Moon Cakes
- Gluten-Free Walnut Raisin Cookies
- Apple Upside Down Cakes

Strawberry Toaster Pastry

Prep Time: 25 minutes

Cook Time: 20 minutes

Servings: 4

INSTRUCTIONS

Crust

2 cups almond flour

2 cage-free eggs

1/4 cup coconut oil (or ghee, cacao butter or coconut butter, softened)

1 tablespoon date butter (or honey or agave)

1/4 teaspoon baking soda

1/4 teaspoon vanilla

1/2 teaspoon Celtic sea salt

Filling

2 cups chopped strawberries (about 3/4 pint whole strawberries) (fresh or frozen)

2 tablespoons raw honey (or agave)

1/2 teaspoon vanilla

1/4 teaspoon Celtic sea salt

INSTRUCTIONS

1. Preheat oven to 400 degrees. Line sheet pan with parchment or baking mat. Cover cutting board with parchment.

2. For *Crust*, sift almond flour into medium mixing bowl. Add baking soda, vanilla and salt.
3. In a small mixing bowl, whisk eggs and date butter. Add flour mixture and mix to combine. Add oil, ghee or butter and mix until malleable dough comes together.
4. Roll in plastic wrap or wrap tightly in parchment and refrigerate for 15 minutes.
5. Heat medium pan over medium heat.
6. Chop strawberries and add to hot pan with honey, vanilla and salt. Cook strawberries down until juices thicken and reduce, about 10 minutes. Stir occasionally.
7. Remove dough from refrigerator. Roll out dough on parchment covered cutting board to about 1/8 inch thick rectangle with rolling pin. Use sharp knife or pizza cutter to cut dough into 4 rectangles.
8. Scoop equal portions of *Filling* into center of one side of each dough rectangle. Fold bare half of dough over filled half. Press edges together, letting any trapped air escape. Crimp edges of dough together with fork. Repeat with remaining dough.
9. Arrange pastries on prepared sheet pan and bake 15 - 20 minutes, or until golden and cooked through.
10. Remove from oven and serve immediately. Or allow to cool and serve room temperature.
11. Reheat in toaster, if preferred.

Gluten-Free Cocoa Zucchini Muffin

Prep Time: 10 minutes

Cook Time: 15 minutes

Servings: 12

INGREDIENTS

1 1/2 cups almond flour

2 cage-free eggs

1 small zucchini (about 1 cup grated)

1/2 cup unsweetened applesauce

1/4 cup date butter (or agave or raw honey)

1/4 cup coconut oil (or cacao or coconut butter, melted)

1/4 cup cocoa powder

2 tablespoons ground chia seed (or flax meal)

1 teaspoon baking soda

1 teaspoon baking powder

1 teaspoon vanilla

1 teaspoon ground cinnamon

1 teaspoon ground black pepper

1/2 teaspoon Celtic sea salt

1/4 cup cocoa nibs or chocolate chips (optional)

INSTRUCTIONS

1. Preheat oven to 350 degrees F. Line muffin pan with paper liners or lightly coat with coconut oil.

2. Add eggs, oil or melted butter, applesauce and date butter to food processor or high-speed blender. Process until thick, light mixture forms, about 1 - 2 minutes.
3. Sift almond flour, cocoa powder, chia or flax meal, baking soda and powder, salt and spices into processor. Process to combine, about 1 minute.
4. Grate zucchini and stir in with cocoa nibs or chocolate chips (optional).
5. Use scoop or tablespoon to pour batter into prepared muffin pan. Bake for about 15 - 20 minutes, until toothpick inserted into center comes out clean.
6. Remove from oven and let cool about 5 minutes.
7. Serve warm. Or let cool completely and serve room temperature.

Vanilla Bean Shortbread Cookies

Prep Time: 5 minutes

Cook Time: 20 minutes

Servings: 12

INGREDIENTS

1 2/3 cups almond flour

2/3 cup almonds (blanched, skinless)

1/4 cup coconut oil (or cacao butter or coconut butter, melted)

1/4 cup date butter (or raw honey or agave)

1 Madagascar whole vanilla bean

1/4 teaspoon baking soda

1/4 teaspoon Celtic sea salt (plus extra)

INSTRUCTIONS

1. Preheat oven to 300 degrees F. Line sheet pan with parchment or baking mat.
2. Add almonds to food processor or high-speed blender and process until finely ground, about 2 minutes.
3. Add ground almonds to medium mixing bowl. Sift in almond flour, baking soda and salt.
4. Split vanilla bean pod in half and scrap insides into small mixing bowl. Add oil or melted butter and date butter. Mix to combine.
5. Pour vanilla mixture into flour mixture and mix to form dough.

6. Use mini ice cream scoop or tablespoon to drop portions of dough onto prepared sheet pan. Bake for 20 minutes , or until lightly browned.
7. Remove from oven and let cool at least 5 minutes.
8. Serve warm. Or let cool completely and serve room temperature.

Cranberry Pistachio Biscotti

Prep Time: 15 minutes
Cook Time: 45 minutes*
Servings: 6

INGREDIENTS

1 cup almond flour
1/2 cup coconut flour
1/2 cup raw honey (or date butter or agave)
1/4 cup pistachios
1/4 cup dried cranberries
1/2 teaspoon vanilla
1/2 teaspoon baking soda
1/4 teaspoon Celtic sea salt

INSTRUCTIONS

1. Preheat oven to 350 degrees F. Line sheet pan with parchment paper. Heat medium pan over medium heat.
2. In medium mixing bowl, blend almond flour, coconut flour, baking soda and salt with hand mixer or whisk.
3. Beat in honey and vanilla until well combined and thick, sticky dough forms. Mix in pistachios and cranberries with wooden spoon.
4. Form dough into flattened, uniform mound about 1 inch thick on sheet pan. Pat down mound to keep any nuts from sticking out.

5. Bake for about 15 minutes. Remove from oven and allow to cool for about 15 minutes.
6. Use a very sharp serrated knife to carefully cut biscotti log into 1/2 - 2/3 inch slices. Hold on to the mound and cut on a diagonal. If it becomes crumbly, stick it back together.
7. Lay slices on their sides and return to oven for 15 minutes.
8. *Turn oven off and leave oven door open a crack. Allow biscotti to cool and dry for at least 2 hours.
9. Serve room temperature.

Gluten-Free Cherry Pie

Prep Time: 30 minutes

Cook Time: 40 minutes

Servings: 12

INGREDIENTS

Crust

3 1/2 cups almond flour

2 cage-free eggs

1/2 cup coconut oil (or cacao butter or ghee)

1/2 cup nut milk (or water)

1/4 teaspoon Celtic sea salt

Filling

2 cups pitted cherries (fresh or frozen)

3/4 cup raw honey (or agave or date butter)

1/4 cup tapioca flour

1 tablespoon coconut oil (or cacao or coconut butter)

1/2 teaspoon vanilla

INSTRUCTIONS

1. *For *Crust*, blend almond flour and salt in small mixing bowl. Add eggs, oil or butter, and nut milk. Mix until dough forms, then divide. Roll half of dough into a round disc that will fit over pie pan, then cover with parchment paper. Press remaining dough into pie pan. Refrigerate dough for 30 minutes.

2. For *Filling*, add cherries, sweetener, coconut and vanilla to medium pot. Sift in tapioca and stir to combine. Heat pot over low heat and bring to simmer, about 10 - 15 minutes. Stir occasionally.
3. Once juice releases from cherries, increase heat to medium and bring to a boil, about 5 minutes. Stir frequently. Cook until juice reduces and mixture thickens, about 5 - 8 minutes. Remove from heat and set aside in refrigerator to cool.
4. Preheat oven to 375 degrees F.
5. Remove dough from refrigerator. Pour *Filling* into bottom *Crust*. Use pizza cutter or sharp knife to cut 1 inch strips from dough disc. Cover pie with dough strips in lattice (crisscross) formation. Press edges of dough together to create seal.
6. Bake about 40 minutes, until dough is golden brown and *Filling* is set.
7. Remove from oven and let cool about 20 minutes.
8. Slice and serve warm. Or let cool completely and serve room temperature.

Berry Cobbler

Prep Time: 5 minutes

Cook Time: 25 minutes

Servings: 8

INGREDIENTS

1 cup blueberries

1 cup raspberries

1 cup strawberries (chopped)

1 cup blackberries

2 tablespoons tapioca flour (or arrowroot powder)

1 teaspoon vanilla

1/2 teaspoon ground ginger

1/4 teaspoon Celtic sea salt

Crumble

1 cup almond flour

1/2 cup almonds

1/4 cup coconut oil (or cacao butter)

1/4 cup almond butter

1/4 cup dried pitted dates

1 teaspoon vanilla

1/2 teaspoon ground cinnamon

1/2 teaspoon Celtic sea salt

Raw honey (or agave or date butter) (optional)

INSTRUCTIONS

1. Preheat oven to 350 degrees F. Lightly coat sides of baking dish with coconut oil.
2. Add berries, vanilla, ginger and salt to medium mixing bowl. Sift tapioca into bowl and gently toss. Transfer to prepared baking dish and set aside.
3. For *Crumble*, add dates, oil or butter, and almonds to food processor or high-speed blender. Pulse until dates and almonds are finely chopped or coarsely ground.
4. Transfer to clean medium mixing bowl with almond flour, almond butter, vanilla, cinnamon and salt. Mix with hands or wooden spoon until crumbly mixture resembling moist graham cracker crust forms. Add sweetener to reach desired consistency, if necessary.
5. Sprinkle crumble evenly over berries and bake about 25 minutes, until crumble is golden brown and crisp.
6. Remove from oven and let cool about 5 minutes.
7. Serve warm. Or let cool completely and serve room temperature.

Vanilla Peach Cake

Prep Time: 10 minutes
Cook Time: 50 minutes
Servings: 12

INGREDIENTS

4 ripe peaches
3/4 cup coconut flour
10 cage-free eggs
1/2 cup coconut oil (or cacao or coconut butter)
1/3 cup raw honey (or agave, date butter or stevia)
2 tablespoons tapioca flour (or arrowroot powder)
1 teaspoon baking soda
1 1/2 teaspoons vanilla
1 teaspoon Celtic sea salt

INSTRUCTIONS

1. Preheat oven to 350 degrees F. Line square or rectangular baking dish with parchment paper, or coat with coconut oil.
2. Slice peaches in half, twist to release from pit and remove pit. Dice 2 peaches and set aside.
3. Roughly chop remaining peaches and add to food processor or high-speed blender. Process until almost smooth, about 1 minute.
4. Add eggs, oil or butter, and flour to processor in 2 batches. Process until well combined, about 1 - 2 minutes. Add sweetener, baking

soda, vanilla and salt. Process until light, thick batter forms. Stir in diced peaches.

5. Pour batter into prepared baking pan and bake about 50 minutes, until golden brown and toothpick inserted into center comes out moist but clean.
6. Remove from oven and let cool about 10 minutes.
7. Slice and serve warm. Or let cool completely and serve room temperature or warm.

Lemon Bundt Cake

Prep Time: 15 minutes

Cook Time: 45 minutes

Servings: 12

INGREDIENTS

6 cage-free eggs

1 cup almond flour

3 large lemons

1/2 cup raw honey (or agave or date butter)

1/4 cup coconut oil (cacao or coconut butter, melted)

2 teaspoons baking soda

1 teaspoon vanilla

1/2 teaspoon Celtic sea salt

INSTRUCTIONS

1. Preheat oven to 350 degrees F. Coat Bundt pan with coconut oil.
2. Add eggs to food processor or high-speed blender. Process until pale and lightened, about 2 minutes.
3. Zest 1 lemon, then juice all lemons into processor. Add flour, sweetener, oil or butter, baking soda, vanilla and salt. Process until well combined, about 1 - 2 minutes.
4. Pour batter into prepared Bundt pan and bake about 45 minutes, until golden brown and toothpick inserted halfway between center and edge of pan comes out clean.

5. Remove oven and let cool 15 minutes. Turn cake out onto serving dish.
6. Slice and serve warm. Or allow to cool completely and serve room temperature.

Chocolate Zucchini Cake

Prep Time: 10 minutes

Cook Time: 25 minutes

Servings: 12

INGREDIENTS

1 1/2 cups almond flour

2 cage-free eggs

1 medium zucchini (1 1/2 cups grated)

1/2 cup unsweetened applesauce

1/4 cup coconut oil

1/4 - 1/2 cup sweetener*

1/4 cup cocoa powder

2 tablespoons ground chia seed (or flax meal)

1 teaspoon baking soda

1 teaspoon baking powder

1 teaspoon vanilla

1 teaspoon ground cinnamon

1 teaspoon ground black pepper

1/2 teaspoon sea salt

1/4 cup cocoa nibs or chocolate chips (optional)

INSTRUCTIONS

1. Preheat oven to 350 degrees F. Line rectangular baking pan with parchment or lightly coat with coconut oil.

2. Add eggs, coconut oil, applesauce and sweetener to food processor or bullet blender. Process until mixture is thick and lightened.
3. Grate zucchini and add to medium mixing bowl. Pour egg mixture over grated zucchini.
4. Sift almond flour, cocoa powder, chia meal, baking soda and powder, salt and spices into bowl. Beat with hand mixer or whisk to combine. Stir in cocoa nibs or chocolate chips (optional).
5. Pour batter into prepared baking pan and bake for about 25 minutes, until toothpick inserted into center comes out clean.
6. Remove from oven and let cool about 10 minutes.
7. Slice and serve warm. Or let cool completely and serve room temperature.

stevia, raw honey or agave nectar

Ginger Spice Cookies

Prep Time: 15 minutes

Cook Time: 15 minutes

Servings: 6

INGREDIENTS

1 1/2 cups almond flour

1 cage-free egg

1/4 cup sweetener*

2 tablespoons coconut oil

1 teaspoon ground chia seed (or flax meal)

1/4 teaspoon baking soda

1 tablespoon ground ginger

1/2 teaspoon ground clove

Pinch all spice

Pinch ground black pepper

Pinch sea salt

INSTRUCTIONS

1. Preheat oven to 350 degrees F. Line sheet pan with parchment or baking mat, or lightly coat with coconut oil.
2. Beat egg, oil, sweetener and chia meal in medium mixing bowl with hand mixer or whisk.
3. Add almond flour, baking soda, salt and spices. Mix until combined.
4. Chill batter in freezer for 5 - 10 minutes.

5. Scoop chilled batter into 6 large rounds on prepared sheet pan. Press into disk shape with hand.
6. Bake for about 15 minutes, until firm around the edges and golden brown.
7. Remove from oven and let cool about 10 minutes.
8. Serve warm. Or let cool completely and serve room temperature.

raw honey, agave nectar, grade B maple syrup, molasses

Orange Cranberry Muffins

Prep Time: 5 minutes
Cook Time: 20 minutes
Servings: 12

INGREDIENTS

1 1/2 cups almond flour

2 cage-free eggs

1/2 cup fresh squeezed orange juice (about 2 oranges)

1/4 cup coconut oil

1/4 cup dried cranberries

1 tablespoon orange zest

1 teaspoon baking powder

1/2 teaspoon vanilla

1/2 teaspoon sea salt

INSTRUCTIONS

1. Preheat oven to 350 degrees F. Line muffin pan with paper liners or coconut oil.
2. In medium bowl, beat eggs with hand mixer or whisk until light and a foamy. Add coconut oil, orange juice and zest. Beat well.
3. Sift in almond flour, baking powder, vanilla and salt. Mix until combined. Stir in cranberries.
4. Use ice cream scoop or tablespoon to scoop batter into prepared muffin pan.

5. Bake about 20 minutes, or until toothpick inserted into center comes out clean.
6. Remove from oven and serve warm. Or let cool completely and serve room temperature.

NOTE: Bake in oiled loaf pan for 40 - 45 minutes for **Cranberry Orange Bread**.

stevia, raw honey or agave nectar

Milano Cookie Sandwiches

Prep Time: 30 minutes

Cook Time: 15 minutes

Servings: 12

INGREDIENTS

Lady Fingers

1/3 cup coconut flour

3 tablespoons arrowroot powder

4 eggs

1/4 cup sweetener*

1/2 teaspoon baking powder

1/2 teaspoon vanilla

Chocolate Filling

4 oz organic dark chocolate

2 oz full-fat coconut milk

INSTRUCTIONS

1. Preheat oven to 400 degrees F. Line two sheet pans with parchment paper. Fit pastry bag with 1/2 inch round tip, or cut 1/4 inch corner off sturdy kitchen storage bag (like Ziploc®).
2. For *Lady Fingers*, beat egg yolks, sweetener and vanilla until thick and pale.
3. In separate bowl, beat egg whites to stiff peaks with hand mixer or whisk, about 8 minutes. Fold half of egg whites into egg yolk

mixture. Then sift in coconut flour, arrowroot powder and baking powder. Fold in remaining egg whites.
4. Scoop batter into pastry or storage bag. Place in tall wide contain and fold open end of bag over edge of container for easier prep.
5. Pipe 4 inch cookies onto prepared sheet pans about 2 inches apart.
6. Place in oven and bake for 8 minutes, until set and just golden.
7. Remove cookies from oven and transfer full parchment sheet onto wire rack to cool completely. Do not try to remove warm cookies from parchment.
8. Heat 1 inch water in bottom of double boiler, or in bottom pan with metal or class bowl on top.
9. For Chocolate Filling, melt chocolate and coconut milk over double boiler until smooth.
10. Remove cooled *Lady Fingers* from parchment. Dip bottom of cookie in melted chocolate and press against bottom of second cookie to make sandwich. Repeat with remaining cookies.
11. Serve warm. Let chocolate set for 10 minutes, in refrigerator if preferred, and serve chilled or room temperature.

stevia, raw honey or agave nectar

Cocoa Spice Pinwheel Cookies

Prep Time: 10 minutes

Cook Time: 20 minutes

Servings: 12

INGREDIENTS

2 cups almond flour

2 tablespoon sweetener*

1 egg

1 teaspoon vanilla

1/2 teaspoon baking powder

1/4 teaspoon sea salt

Filling

2 tablespoons cocoa powder

2 tablespoons sweetener*

2 teaspoons ground cinnamon

1 teaspoon ground black pepper

1/2 teaspoon vanilla

INSTRUCTIONS

1. Preheat oven to 300 degrees F. Line sheet pan with parchment or baking mat. Prepare 2 additional sheets of parchment.
2. Add flour, egg, sweetener, vanilla, baking powder and salt to medium bowl. Blend with wooden spoon, then knead with hand to form thick dough.

3. Divide dough in half. Place half of dough in small mixing bowl. Add all *Filling* ingredients to bowl and mix until well combined.
4. Roll out each half of dough separately on parchment sheets. Roll into equal rectangles.
5. Place *Filling* rectangle on top of plain dough. Use parchment to help roll dough tightly along long edge into log.
6. Use sharp knife to cut log into 1/4 round slices. Place cookies on prepared sheet pan and bake about 10 minutes, until edges are golden brown.
7. Remove from oven and let cool about 5 minutes.
8. Serve warm. Or let cool completely and serve room temperature.

raw honey, agave nectar or maple syrup

Key Lime Coconut Bars

Prep Time: 15 minutes

Cook Time: 30 minutes

Servings: 12

INGREDIENTS

Crust

1/2 cup raw cashews

2/3 cup coconut flour

2 eggs

2 tablespoons coconut oil

2 tablespoons sweetener*

1 tablespoon flaked or shredded coconut

1 teaspoon fresh lime juice

1/2 teaspoon baking soda

1/2 teaspoon vanilla

Filling

2 eggs

2 egg yolks

1 cup fresh key lime juice or (about 12 key limes - sub 10 Persian limes)

1/2 cup sweetener*

1/3 - 1/2 cup flaked or shredded coconut

2 tablespoons coconut flour

1 teaspoon lime zest

INSTRUCTIONS

1. Preheat oven to 350 degrees F. Lightly coat rectangular baking dish with coconut oil, or line with parchment.
2. For *Crust*, add cashews and coconut to food processor or bullet blender and process until finely ground. Add remaining *Crust* ingredients to food processor and pulse until dough comes together.
3. Press dough into bottom of baking dish, and slightly up the sides. Dock crust with fork to prevent bubbling.
4. Place crust in oven and bake for 8 - 10 minutes.
5. For *Filling*, beat together eggs, egg yolks, lime juice, lime zest and sweetener with hand mixer or whisk in medium bowl.
6. Sift in coconut flour and beat to combine. Let mixture sit for 5 minutes. Add coconut and beat again.
7. Pour *Filling* over par baked crust. Place in oven and bake 20 minutes, until center is set but still jiggles slightly.
8. Remove from oven and let cool for 20 minutes. Refrigerate about 20 minutes, until fully set and chilled.
9. Serve chilled or room temperature.

* *raw honey or agave nectar*

Coconut Baked Donut

Prep Time: 5 minutes

Cook Time: 20 minutes

Servings: 6

INGREDIENTS

Donuts

1 3/4 cups almond flour

1 tablespoon coconut flour

2 eggs

1/3 cup coconut oil

1/4 cup unsweetened applesauce

1/4 cup sweetener*

2 tablespoons nut milk

2 teaspoons vanilla

3/4 teaspoon baking soda

1/2 teaspoon sea salt

Topping

1/2 cup flaked or shredded coconut

1/4 cup full-fat coconut milk

2 tablespoon sweetener

1/4 teaspoon vanilla

INSTRUCTIONS

1. Preheat oven to 350 degreesF. Lightly coat donut pan with coconut oil.
2. Add almond and coconut flours, baking soda and salt to food processor or high-speed blender. Process for 1 minute.
3. Add eggs, sweetener, coconut oil, applesauce, nut milk and vanilla. Process until light, thick batter forms, about 1 - 2 minutes.
4. Pour batter into donut pan until wells are 3/4 full.
5. Place in oven and bake for about 20 minutes, until dough is set and lightly browned.
6. For *Topping*, combine coconut milk, sweetener and vanilla in small mixing bowl.
7. Remove pan from oven at let cool about 5 minutes. Then remove donuts from pan.
8. Dip donuts in coconut icing then sprinkle with flaked or shredded coconut.
9. Transfer decorated donuts to serving dish.
10. Serve warm. Or let cool completely and serve room temperature.

NOTE: Bake in 8 mini cake pans or specialty cake pop pans lightly coated with coconut oil for fillable donuts or donut holes if you do not have a donut pan.

* *stevia, raw honey or agave nectar*

Soft Pumpkin Cookies

Prep Time: 15 minutes

Cook Time: 20 minutes

Servings: 15

INGREDIENTS

Sweet Potato Cookies

1 cup almond flour

3/4 cup organic pumpkin purée

1/4 cup full-fat coconut milk

1 egg

1 orange

2 tablespoons sweetener*

1/2 teaspoon baking powder

1 teaspoon ground cinnamon

1/4 teaspoon ground ginger

1/4 teaspoon ground nutmeg

1/4 teaspoon ground white pepper (or ground black pepper)

INSTRUCTIONS

1. Preheat oven to 400 degrees F. Line sheet pan with parchment or lightly coat with coconut oil.
2. Zest *then* juice orange into medium mixing bowl. Beat in egg, coconut milk and sweetener with hand mixer or whisk.
3. Sift flour, baking powder and spices into bowl and mix well. Add pumpkin purée and mix to combine.

4. Scoop 15 cookies onto prepared sheet pan. Place in oven for about 20 minutes, until golden and set.
5. Remove and serve warm. Or allow to cool completely and serve room temperature.

raw honey, agave nectar or maple syrup

Asian Orange Muffins

Prep Time: 10 minutes

Cook Time: 15 minutes

Servings: 12

INGREDIENTS

1 1/2 cups almond flour

2 eggs

1 1/2 cups grated carrot

1/4 cup coconut oil

1/4 cup unsweetened applesauce

1/2 cup fresh squeezed orange juice

1 tablespoon orange zest

1 tablespoon grated fresh ginger

1 tablespoon ground ginger

1 teaspoon vanilla

1 teaspoon baking soda

1 teaspoon baking powder

1/2 teaspoon sea salt

INSTRUCTIONS

1. Preheat oven to 350 degrees F. Line muffin pan with paper liners or coconut oil.
2. Peel ginger. Grate ginger and carrots. In medium bowl beat eggs with hand mixer or whisk until light and a bit frothy. Add oil,

applesauce, orange juice and zest. Beat well. Fold in carrots and ginger.
3. Sift and stir in flour, baking soda and powder, spices and salt until combined.
4. Use ice cream scoop or tablespoon to scoop batter into muffin tins, about 1/2 - 3/4 full.
5. Bake 15 - 18 minutes, or until toothpick inserted into center comes out clean.
6. Serve warm or room temperature.

NOTE: Bake in oiled loaf pan for 35 - 45 minutes for **Asian Orange Bread**.

stevia, raw honey or agave nectar

Coconut Crisps

Prep Time: 10 minutes

Cook Time: 10 minutes

Servings: 4

INGREDIENTS

1 cup coconut flour

3/4 cup almond flour

4 egg whites

1/4 cup coconut oil

1/4 cup coconut crème

1/4 cup sweetener

1/2 cup flaked coconut

1 teaspoon vanilla

1/2 teaspoon baking soda

3/4 teaspoon sea salt

1/2 teaspoon ground white pepper (or black pepper)

INSTRUCTIONS

1. Preheat oven to 375 degrees F. Line sheet pan with parchment paper or coat with coconut oil. Prepare two additional sheets of parchment.
2. Whisk egg and oil with hand mixer or whisk until blended and slightly frothy. Add sweetener, coconut crème and vanilla, and continue blending.

3. Sift in half of flour, baking soda, vanilla, salt and pepper. Add coconut flakes. Sift in remaining flour. Stir and bring dough together.
4. Form dough into rectangle and flatten with hands on parchment. Cover with second sheet of parchment and flatten to about 1/4 inch with rolling pin. Remove top layer of parchment.
5. Cut rectangles from dough with pizza cutter or sharp knife. Carefully flip dough onto sheet pan. Arrange at least 1/2 inch apart on sheet pan.
6. Bake for about 10 minutes, or until crisp and golden brown. Remove and let cool. Serve room temperature.

Pecan Chess Pies

Prep Time: 20 minutes

Cook Time: 25 minutes

Servings: 6

INGREDIENTS

Crust

1 1/2 cups almond flour

1/2 cup pecans

1 egg

2 tablespoons coconut oil

1/4 teaspoon sea salt

Filling

1 cup full-fat coconut milk

2 cups pecans

1 cup dried pitted dates

1/2 cup sweetener*

2 eggs

2 egg yolks

1 1/2 tablespoons arrowroot powder

2 tablespoons coconut oil

1 teaspoon vanilla

INSTRUCTIONS

1. Preheat oven to 350 degrees F. Coat 6 mini pie plates or pie pans with coconut oil. Bring small pot of water to boil, leaving room for dates.
2. Add dates to boiling water for about 5 - 10 minutes, until tender. Then drain.
3. For *Crust*, process pecans in food processor or bullet lender until well ground. Add to small mixing bowl with almond flour and salt. Mix in oil and egg until dough forms.
4. Press dough into pie plates with hand or wooden spoon. Bake about 10 minutes, until golden. Remove pie shells from oven and set aside.
5. Chop 1 cup pecans and set aside
6. For *Filling*, process softened dates in food processor or bullet blender with about half of coconut milk. Add to medium mixing bowl with remaining coconut milk, sweetener, eggs, egg yolks, coconut oil, vanilla and arrowroot powder. Beat with hand mixer or whisk until combined and a bit airy. Mix in chopped pecans.
7. Pour batter into mini pie crusts. Top with whole pecans and bake for 20 - 25 minutes, until filling is set.
8. Remove pies and let cool about 20 minutes before serving.
9. Serve warm. Or refrigerate and serve cold. Also great at room temperature.

*stevia, raw honey or agave nectar

NOTE: For large **Pecan Chess Pie**, bake in 9-inch pie plate for 45 - 55 minutes, or until center is set.

Mixed Berry Trifle

Prep Time: 10 minutes

Cook Time: 25 minutes

Servings: 12

INGREDIENTS

Cake

1 cup almond flour

1 cup coconut flour

3/4 cup coconut milk

4 eggs

1/2 cup sweetener*

1/2 cup coconut oil

2 tablespoons vanilla

2 teaspoons baking soda

Filling

1 cup coconut cream

2 tablespoons sweetener*

1 cup strawberries

1/2 cup blueberries

1/2 cup raspberries

1/2 cup blackberries

Juice of orange half

Juice of lemon half

Zest of orange half

Zest of lemon half

1/4 cup pistachios

INSTRUCTIONS
1. Preheat oven to 350 degrees F. Line muffin pan with paper liner or coat with coconut oil.
2. In large mixing bowl, beat eggs and coconut milk until light and airy. Beat in sweetener, oil and vanilla.
3. Sift in almond flour, coconut flour and baking soda. Mix until well combined.
4. Use ice cream scoop or spoon to scoop batter into muffin pan. Fill each cup 1/2 - 2/3 full with batter.
5. Bake in for about 15 minutes, until firm but springy in the center.
6. Remove cupcakes from oven and turn out onto wire rack or plate. Allow to cool for about 10 minutes and remove paper liners.
7. Dice strawberries and add to medium bowl with blueberries, raspberries, blackberries, lemon and orange zests and juices. Toss to combine.
8. In small bowl, mixi coconut cream with 2 tablespoon sweetener.
9. Slice cupcake in half to create top and bottom. Dollop coconut cream onto bottom half, then top with a spoonful of fruit. Drain juice from spoon before adding to cake.
10. Place cupcake top on top of fruit. Press down slightly. Add another dollop of coconut cream and another spoonful of fruit. Repeat with remaining cupcakes.
11. Serve room temperature. Or chill for 30 minutes and serve.

NOTE: Bake cake in 3 round cake pans for 20 minutes, then layer with cream and berries and stack for **Mixed Berry Trifle Cake**.

stevia, raw honey or agave nectar

Sugar Cookies

Prep Time: 10 minutes

Cook Time: 15 minutes

Servings: 12

INGREDIENTS

1 1/2 cups almond flour

1 cup coconut flour

1/2 cup sweetener*

5 dried pitted dates

1 egg

2 teaspoons coconut oil

1 teaspoon vanilla

1/2 teaspoon baking soda

Pinch sea salt

Water

INSTRUCTIONS

1. Preheat oven to 350 degrees F. Line sheet pan with parchment paper. Bring small pot of water to boil. Add dates and boil for about 5 - 8 minutes, until softened.
2. Add dates to food processor or bullet blender and process until smooth. Add leftover water if necessary.
3. Add sweetener, egg, oil and vanilla to dates and process until smooth.

4. Add date mixture to medium bowl. Sift in almond flour, coconut flour baking soda and salt. Beat with hand mixer until combined and smooth, about 5 minutes.
5. Roll dough into a log about 3 inches in diameter. Slice into 1/4 inch thick disks.
6. Place disks on sheet pan and bake for about 8 - 10 minutes.
7. Remove form oven and cool for a few minutes.
8. Serve warm or room temperature.

*stevia, raw honey or agave nectar

Apple Dump Muffins

Prep Time: 15 minutes

Cook Time: 25 minutes

Servings: 12

INGREDIENTS

6 medium apples

1 cup almond flour

1/4 cup tapioca flour

3 eggs

1/2 cup coconut oil

1/2 cup sweetener*

2 teaspoons baking powder

2 tablespoons ground cinnamon

1 teaspoon ground nutmeg

1 teaspoon sea salt

1/2 teaspoon black pepper (or white pepper)

Juice of lemon half

INSTRUCTIONS

1. Preheat oven to 350 degrees F. Lightly coat muffin pan with coconut oil, or line with paper liners.
2. Peel, core and thinly slice apples. Add to medium bowl with 1 tablespoon cinnamon and juice of half a lemon. Evenly sprinkle on tapioca flour and carefully toss with hands to coat apples.

3. In medium mixing bowl, blend almond flour, baking powder, spices and salt. Beat in eggs, sweetener and coconut oil with hand mixer or whisk. Fold in sliced apples.
4. Scoop batter into muffin pan and bake for 20 -25 minutes, or until top is browned and firm but springy. A toothpick inserted into the center should come our moist but clean.
5. Serve warm solo, or drizzled with your favorite sweetener.

NOTE: For *Apple Dump Cake*, bake in square baking dish or Bundt pan for 40 - 50 minutes.

raw honey, agave nectar or maple syrup

Fruit And Nut Cake

Prep Time: 10 minutes

Cook Time: 25 minutes

Servings: 8

INGREDIENTS

1 1/2 cup almond flour

4 eggs

2 tablespoons coconut oil

Juice of orange half

1/4 cup sweetener*

1/2 cup walnuts

1/4 cup pecans

1/2 cup dried pitted dates

1/2 cup dried cherries

1/4 cup dried apricots

1/4 cup raisins

1/2 teaspoon baking soda

1 teaspoon ground ginger

1 teaspoon vanilla

1/2 teaspoon sea salt

Zest of orange half

INSTRUCTIONS

1. Preheat oven to 350 degrees F. Lightly coat 2 small loaf pans or one Bundt pan with coconut oil.

2. Sift almond flour, baking soda and salt into large mixing bowl.
3. Chop walnuts, pecans, apricots and dates. Then stir all dried fruit and nuts into flour mixture.
4. In medium mixing bowl, mix eggs, coconut oil, juice and zest of half an orange, sweetener, ginger and vanilla. Then pour and mix into dry ingredients until just combined.
5. Scoop batter into loaf pans or Bundt pan, and smooth tops with spatula.
6. Bake 20 - 30 minutes, or until firm, browned and firm in the center.
7. Remove from oven and allow to cool before slicing.
8. Serve warm or room temperature.

stevia, raw honey or agave nectar

Honey Nut Bun

Prep Time: 15 minutes

Cook Time: 30 minutes

Servings: 4

INGREDIENTS

Bun

1 cup tapioca flour/starch

1/4 - 1/3 cup coconut flour

1 egg

1/2 cup warm water

1/2 cup coconut oil

1 teaspoon apple cider vinegar

1 teaspoon vanilla

1/2 teaspoon cinnamon

1/2 teaspoon baking soda

1/2 teaspoon sea salt

Filling

1 cup walnuts

1/4 cup sweetener*

2 teaspoons cinnamon

1 teaspoon ground ginger

INSTRUCTIONS

1. Preheat oven to 350 degrees F. Line sheet pan with parchment paper or coat with coconut oil. Heat medium skillet over medium-high heat.
2. For *Filling*, mix walnuts, sweetener, cinnamon and ginger in small mixing bowl. Set aside.
3. In medium bowl, sift together tapioca flour, 1/4 cup coconut flour, vanilla, cinnamon, baking soda and salt. Stir in warm water and oil.
4. Whisk egg and vinegar in small bowl. Add egg mixture to flour mixture and mix until well combined.
5. Add 1 tablespoon coconut flour or water at a time if needed to form soft and slightly sticky dough.
6. Divide dough into 4 portions and flatten into round disks. Dust your hand or rolling pin with extra tapioca flour to prevent sticking.
7. Scoop *Filling* into center of dough disks and pinch edges of dough together to create round, sealed ball.
8. Place buns sealed side down on sheet pan and pat down slightly. Bake 20 minutes, or until edges are golden brown and dough is cooked through.
9. Serve immediately. Or store in lidded container.

stevia, raw honey or agave nectar

Orange Anzac Biscuits

Prep Time: 5 minutes

Cook Time: 25 minutes

Servings: 12

INGREDIENTS

3/4 cup almond flour

3/4 cup sliced almonds

3/4 cup flaked or shredded coconut

1/4 cup date butter (raw honey or agave)

1/4 cup coconut oil (or ghee or cacao butter, melted)

1 orange (or tangerine or Clementine)

1/2 teaspoon baking soda

1/4 teaspoon ground ginger

INSTRUCTIONS

1. Preheat oven to 300 degrees F. Line sheet pan with parchment sheet or baking mat.
2. In medium mixing bowl, combine almond flour, sliced almonds and coconut.
3. Zest *then* juice orange into small mixings bowl. Add date butter and oil or melted butter. Mix to combine.
4. Add wet mixture to dry mixture and mix until dough comes together.
5. Form 12 large biscuits with tablespoon or scoop. Place on prepared sheet pan and flatten slightly.

6. Bake for 25 - 30 minutes, until golden. Remove from oven and let cool slightly before serving.
7. Serve warm. Or allow to cool completely and store in airtight container.

Sweet Cherry Fig Newtons

Prep Time: 10 minutes

Cook Time: 15 minutes

Servings: 12

INSTRUCTIONS

Cookie Dough

1 1/2 cups almond flour

1/4 cup dried pitted dates

1/4 cup date butter (or agave or honey)

1/4 cup coconut oil (or cacao or coconut butter, melted)

1 teaspoon vanilla

1/4 teaspoon Celtic sea salt

Cherry Fig Filling

1/2 cup dried black mission figs

1/4 cup pitted cherries (fresh or thawed)

1/4 teaspoon ground ginger

INSTRUCTIONS

1. Preheat oven to 350 degrees F. Line sheet pan with parchment or baking mat.
2. For *Cookie Dough*, Add dried dates, date butter, and oil or melted butter to food processor or high-speed blender. Process until coarsely ground, about 1 - 2 minutes.

3. Sift almond flour and salt into medium mixing bowl. Add date mixture to flour mixture and mix to combine. Set aside.
4. For *Filling*, remove stems from figs and add to clean food processor or high-speed blender with cherries and ginger. Process until smooth mixture forms, about 2 minutes. Set aside.
5. Divide dough in half. Roll first half of dough into long, thin rectangle about 1/4 inch thick between 2 parchment sheets.
6. Spread 1/2 of *Cherry Fig Filling* along one side of the dough, long-ways.
7. Use parchment to fold dough in half along long edge so plain dough covers side with *Cherry Fig Filling*. Dough should resemble flattened log.
8. Press edges of dough together for tight seal. Place on prepared sheet pan. Repeat with remaining *Cookie Dough* and *Cherry Fig Filling*.
9. Bake for 12 - 15 minutes, or until the edges are golden brown.
10. Remove from the oven and let cool about 5 minutes. Then slice logs into 2 inch cookies.
11. Serve immediately. Or allow to cool completely and serve room temperature.

Pineapple Upside Down Cake

Prep Time: 20 minutes

Cook Time: 4 hours

Servings: 8

INGREDIENTS

1 can (20 oz) organic pineapple rings (in juice)

2 cage-free eggs

1 cup almond flour

1/4 cup coconut flour

2 tablespoons tapioca flour (or arrow root powder)

1/2 cup coconut milk (optional)

1/4 cup coconut oil

1/4 cup date butter (or raw honey or agave)

3 tablespoons cacao butter (or coconut butter, softened)

1/2 teaspoon baking soda

1/2 teaspoon baking powder

1 teaspoon vanilla

1/4 teaspoon Celtic sea salt

INSTRUCTIONS

1. Spread softened butter over bottom of slow cooker. Then spread date butter over bottom of slow cooker. Place pineapple slices in bottom of slow cooker.
2. Place remaining pineapple and juice into food processor or high-speed blender. Process until smooth, about 30 seconds.

3. Add eggs, coconut oil, almond flour, coconut flour, tapioca flour, baking soda, baking powder, vanilla and salt to processor. Process until smooth batter forms, about 1 - 2 minutes.
4. Spoon batter into pineapple, filling in any gaps between fruit and slow cooker bottom.
5. Cover slow cooker with tea towel, then with lid. Turn on to high and cook 45 minutes. Decrease temperature to low and cook 3 - 4 hours, until cooked through but still moist.
6. Turn off slow cooker and carefully remove lid. Carefully remove slow cooker dish let cool at least 20 minutes.
7. Invert cake onto serving dish. Slice and serve warm.
8. Or let cool completely and serve room temperature.

Simple Chinese Moon Cakes

Prep Time: 5 minutes*
Cook Time: 15 minutes
Servings: 12

INGREDIENTS

2/3 cup coconut flour
2 cage-free egg yolks
1/2 cup ghee (or cacao or coconut butter)
1/4 cup date butter (or agave or raw honey)

Filling
1 cup dried fruit (apricots, strawberries, blueberries, etc.)
Water

INSTRUCTIONS

1. Preheat oven to 375 degrees F. Cover sheet pan with parchment or baking mat.
2. In medium mixing bowl, cream ghee, sweetener and 1 egg yolk with hand mixer or wooden spoon. Add flour and mix until dough comes together.
3. *Wrap dough in plastic wrap or parchment and refrigerate 30 minutes.
4. For *Filling*, add dried apricots to clean food processor or high-speed blender. Process until thick jam forms, about 1 - 2 minutes. Add enough water to reach desired consistency.

5. Remove dough from refrigerator. Form 24 balls from dough and place on prepared sheet pan. Press thumb into each ball to create indent.
6. Fill each indent with *Filling*. Add remaining egg yolk and 1 teaspoon water to small mixing bowl and brush each *Moon Cake* with egg wash.
7. Bake 15 - 20 minutes, until edges are slightly browned.
8. Remove from oven and let cool about 5 minutes.
9. Serve warm. Or transfer to wire rack to cool completely and serve room temperature.

Gluten-Free Walnut Raisin Cookies

Prep Time: 10 minutes

Cook Time: 15 minutes

Servings: 12

INGREDIENTS

1 1/4 cups almond flour

1 cage-free egg

1/4 cup coconut oil (or cacao or coconut butter)

1/4 cup raw honey (or agave or date butter)

1/4 cup cashew butter

1/2 cup walnuts

1/4 cup raisins

1 teaspoon baking powder

1 teaspoon vanilla

1/4 teaspoon Celtic sea salt

INSTRUCTIONS

1. Preheat oven to 350 degrees F. Line sheet pan with parchment or baking mat.
2. Sift flour, baking powder and salt into medium mixing bowl. Beat with whisk or hand mixer to lighten. Add egg, oil or butter, sweetener, cashew butter, vanilla and salt. Mix well to form dough.
3. Chop walnuts and add to bowl with raisins. Mix to combine.

4. Shape dough into 12 balls and place onto prepared baking sheet. Flatten slightly with hand or spatula.
5. Place in oven and bake 10 - 15 minutes, until golden brown along edges.
6. Remove from oven and let cool 5 minutes.
7. Serve warm. Or transfer to wire rack to cool completely and serve room temperature.

Apple Upside Down Cakes

Prep Time: 5 minutes

Cook Time: 15 minutes

Servings: 2

INGREDIENTS

1 3/4 cups almond meal

2 eggs

3/4 cup almond milk

2 tablespoons sweetener*

1 teaspoon baking powder

Juice of 1/2 lemon

1 teaspoon vanilla

1 teaspoon ground cinnamon

1 teaspoon ground nutmeg

1/4 teaspoon salt

1 tart apple

1/2 cup crushed pecans

INSTRUCTIONS

1. Heat large skillet over medium-high heat and lightly coat with coconut oil.
2. In medium bowl combine lemon juice, vanilla, cinnamon and nutmeg.
3. Peel and core apple, then slice in half length-wise. Lay halves down on flat side and slice thinly from top of apple to bottom.

Carefully toss apple slices in lemon juice and spices. Try not to break any.
4. Arrange apple slices into a circle by overlapping at the bottom and fanning out. Try to make at least 4 circles.
5. Add eggs and almond milk into leftover lemon juice and spices and whisk until combined. Add almond flour, salt and baking powder. Whisk until smooth.
6. Use oiled spatula to lift apples, keeping their arrangement, and place into hot pan. Get at least two apple arrangements into pan together. Sprinkle chopped pecans into pan around apple circles.
7. Use ladle or dry measure cup to pour 1/3 cup of batter over and around apple arrangements in skillet. Do not let pancakes touch as they spread.
8. Cook until sides of pancakes are firm and batter bubbles up a bit. About 3 - 4 minutes.
9. Flip pancakes with spatula, careful not to disturb apples. Cook for additional minute, or until cooked through. Repeat with remaining batter. Re-oil pan if necessary.
10. Pancakes will be slightly delicate, so flip and plate with care.
11. Sprinkle with cinnamon. Serve warm.

stevia, raw honey, or agave nectar

Vegetarian Cookbook

Table of Contents

Gluten-Free Spicy Kale Quiche

Eggplant with Pesto Topping

Spicy Zucchini Eggplant Dine

Lettuce Nut Salad

Eggplant with Red Sauce

Sweet Potatoes Roast

Pepper Quiche

"Green Bean" Casserole

Mushroom Masala

Gluten-Free Matzo Ball Soup

Butternut Squash Soup

Mexican Tomato Soup

Creamy "Cheesy" Broccoli Soup

Pita Bites

Simple Gazpacho + Tortilla Chips

Grain-Free Tortillas

Veggie Burger

Soft Burger Buns

Egg Salad Sandwich

Sandwich Bread

Kelp Noodle Salad

Zucchini Salad with Sundried Tomato Sauce

Quick Raw Avocado Slaw

Vegetarian Texas Chili

Caesar Salad

Spiced Walnut Autumn Salad

Pecan Apricot Spinach Salad

Southern Style Egg Salad

Pesto Tomato Caprese

Cashew Crunch Kelp Noodle Salad

Dill Stuffed Tomatoes

Squash Blossom Stuffers

Indian Egg Fried Rice

Gluten-Free Spicy Kale Quiche

Prep time: 10 minutes
Cook time: 15 minutes
Serves: 4

INGREDIENTS

8 cage-free eggs
2 tbsp extra virgin olive oil
1 7oz bag of Kale greens
1 shallot
¼ tsp chipotle chili pepper powder
2 cloves garlic
½ lemon
2 tbsp coconut oil
¼ tbsp ground black pepper

INSTRUCTIONS

1. Place a steamer basket in the bottom of a large pot and fill with water; if you see water rise above the bottom of the basket, pour some out. Bring the water to a boil.
2. Wash the kale and remove the stems. Mince the garlic and shallot and squeeze the juice from the lemon into a bowl.
3. In a large pan, add the eggs and extra virgin olive oil. Mixing in the chipotle chili pepper powder, scramble the eggs, breaking them up until they form many small pieces, tender yet firm.
4. Place the kale in the pot and steam until tender and bright-green.

5. Remove the kale from the pot and combine with the eggs. Add the garlic, shallot and lemon juice, drizzle the coconut oil over top and add the ground black pepper. Mix and stir thoroughly.
6. Serve immediately or chill 20 minutes and then serve.

Eggplant with Pesto Topping

Prep time: 10 minutes
Cook time: 8 minutes
Serves: 4

INGREDIENTS

1 large, thick eggplant
6-8 tomatoes
4 tbsp olive oil
¼ cup fresh basil
2 cloves garlic

INSTRUCTIONS

1. Preheat the grill. Slice the eggplant lengthwise into ½" thick slices, or ensuring that you have 4 slices. Slice the tomatoes into ¼" thick slices. Combine 4 tbsp olive oil with basil and garlic in a food processor and puree together.
2. Grill the eggplant until browned, turning once, about 3-4 minutes per side.
3. Remove eggplant from the grill and lay the tomato slices out over each piece. Top with the pesto puree and serve.

Spicy Zucchini Eggplant Dine

Prep time: 15 minutes

Cook time: 20 minutes

Serves: 4

INGREDIENTS

3 small zucchini

1 eggplant

2 green peppers

6 tomatoes

1 onion

2 medium carrots

1 four-inch sweet orange pepper

1 cup water

1 tbsp extra virgin olive oil

INSTRUCTIONS

1. Using a julienne peeler, peel zucchini, eggplant and green peppers. Green peppers may be too tough for a julienne peeler, in which case try to simulate the effect of one using a knife. Combine the above in a pan with extra virgin olive oil and saute over medium heat, stirring, for 5 minutes.
2. Meanwhile, cut tomatoes into quarters, carrots into ½" thick slices, dice sweet pepper and dice onion. In a saucepan, combine the above with water and cook over medium heat until carrot is tender,

about 15 minutes. Once finished, blend using an immersion blender, or pour into a blender and puree.
3. Pour the sauce over the zucchini, eggplant and peppers and serve.

Lettuce Nut Salad

Prep time: 10 min

Cook time: 6-8 minutes

Serves: 4

INGREDIENTS

1 7oz bag of Romaine lettuce

1 cup strawberries

1 cup blueberries

1 cup kiwi

½ cup almonds

½ cup walnuts

2 cups coconut milk

1 tbsp arrowroot

1 tsp cinnamon

¼ tsp chipotle chili pepper powder

INSTRUCTIONS

1. Dice the fruits. In a saucepan, combine coconut milk, arrowroot, cinnamon and chipotle chili pepper powder over medium heat. Cook, stirring, for 4 minutes. Add the walnuts and almonds to the sauce and continue cooking until slightly thick.
2. Combine lettuce and fruit in a bowl and drizzle the sauce over the top. Serve immediately or chill 20 minutes and then serve.

Eggplant with Red Sauce

Prep time: 10 minutes
Cook time: 8 minutes
Serves: 2

INGREDIENTS

½ large eggplant cut lengthwise

4 asparagus stalks

2 cloves garlic

1 yellow tomato

2 tsp fresh cilantro

2 tbsp extra virgin olive oil

1 cup organic red sauce

INSTRUCTIONS

1. In a medium saucepan, heat the red sauce on low and keep hot.
2. Slice the eggplant into ½ inch slices, 8 slices total. Heat 1 ½ extra virgin olive oil in a frying pan on medium heat. Cook the eggplant two minutes on one side and another two minutes on the other side. Transfer to a plate.
3. Add ½ tbsp to the pan. Slice the garlic. Rinse the asparagus and cut each asparagus stalk into 3 equal lengths.
4. Add garlic and asparagus to pan and sautee until asparagus is tender.
5. Dice yellow tomato and cilantro and mix together.

6. Place four slices of eggplant on each plate. Spoon red sauce over each slice. Cover with tomato/cilantro mixture and evenly distribute asparagus and garlic cloves.
7. Serve.

Sweet Potatoes Roast

Prep time: 10 minutes

Cook time: 30 minutes

INGREDIENTS

3 sweet potatoes

¼ cup extra virgin olive oil

¼ tsp Celtic sea salt

¼ tsp smoked paprika

INSTRUCTIONS

1. Preheat oven to 500 degrees.
2. Peel the potatoes and cut them into small wedges. In a large bowl, combine potato wedges, extra virgin olive oil, Celtic sea salt and smoked paprika. Mix well until all wedges are coated in all ingredients.
3. Place on a baking sheet and bake for 30 minutes, turning once halfway through, and continue cooking until they are well browned.
4. Remove from oven and let cool. Serve.

Pepper Quiche

Prep time: 5 minutes

Cook time: 3-6 minutes

INGREDIENTS

2 cage-free eggs

1 small onion

1 clove garlic

½ red bell pepper

1 tbsp extra virgin olive oil

¼ tsp smoked paprika

¼ tsp ground black pepper

INSTRUCTIONS
1. Finely chop onion, garlic and red bell pepper.
2. Pour extra virgin olive oil into a pan over medium heat.
3. Crack eggs and pour into a small bowl. Combine with onion, garlic and red bell pepper and whisk until mixed together.
4. Pour contents of bowl into pan and add smoked paprika and ground black pepper. Scramble until desired doneness.
5. Serve.

"Green Bean" Casserole

Prep Time: 5 minutes
Cook Time: 20 minutes
Servings: 12

INGREDIENTS

Casserole

4 cups asparagus

2 cups button mushrooms

1 cup nut milk

1/2 cup cegetable stock

2 tablespoons tapioca flour

1 teaspoon ground white pepper (or ground black pepper)

1 teaspoon garlic powder

1 teaspoon onion powder

Crispy Onions

1/2 cup almond meal

1/2 medium onion (yellow or white)

1 cage-free egg

1 teaspoon paprika

1 teaspoon onion powder

1/4 teaspoon ground black pepper

1 teaspoon Celtic sea salt

Coconut oil (for cooking)

INSTRUCTIONS

1. Preheat oven to 350 degrees F. Bring medium pot of water plus 1/2 teaspoon salt to a boil.
2. For *Casserole*, cut asparagus stalks into quarters. Add to boiling water for about 3 - 4 minutes, until tender but not mushy. Drain and shock in ice bath to stop cooking an preserve color. Set aside.
3. Add tapioca flour and vegetable stock to large pan and heat over medium-high heat. Whisk until smooth, then add nut milk, white pepper, garlic and onion powder.
4. Slice mushrooms and add to pan. Stir and thicken about 8 minutes, until thick and creamy.
5. Add asparagus to pan and stir to coat. Pour into baking or casserole dish and bake about 20 minutes, until heated through. Remove from oven and let cool BOUT 5 minutes.
6. Heat medium pan on medium-high heat and coat with coconut oil.
7. For *Crispy Onions*, whisk egg in medium bowl. In shallow dish, mix almond meal with spices.
8. Peel and slice onion. Toss onions in beaten egg, then in seasoned almond meal to coat. Add to hot oiled pan and fry until crispy and golden brown, about 1 - 2 minutes.
9. Drain *Crispy Onions* on paper towel, then sprinkle over *Casserole*. Serve warm.

Mushroom Masala

Prep Time: 10 minutes
Cook Time: 25 minutes
Servings: 8

INGREDIENTS

1 head cauliflower
1 1/2 cups tomato purée (or tomato sauce)
1 pint (2 cups) mushrooms
1 onion
1 chili pepper
1 /2 green bell pepper
1 large garlic clove
1 inch piece fresh ginger
2 teaspoons coriander leaves (optional)
1 teaspoon garam masala
1/2 teaspoon cayenne pepper
1/2 teaspoon ground coriander
1/2 teaspoon Celtic sea salt
3 tablespoons coconut oil or ghee

INSTRUCTIONS

1. Roughly chop cauliflower, then rice cauliflower in food processor, or mince. Add to medium pot with enough water to cover. Heat pot over medium heat and cook until just tender, about 8 minutes. Drain and transfer to serving dish.

2. Heat medium pan over medium heat. Add oil or butter to hot pan.
3. Peel and finely dice onions. Remove seeds, veins and stem from bell pepper and dice. Slice chili pepper. Peel and mince garlic and onion. Add to hot oiled pan and sauté about 5 minutes.
4. Slice mushrooms and add to pan with tomato, salt and spices. Finely chop coriander leaves and add to pan (optional). Sauté and let simmer about 10 - 12 minutes, stirring occasionally.
5. Transfer to serving dish and serve hot with cauliflower rice.

Gluten-Free Matzo Ball Soup

Prep Time: 5 minutes*
Cook Time: 10 minutes
Servings: 6

INGREDIENTS

6 cups vegetable stock
2 cups almond flour
4 cage-free egg yolks
1/4 teaspoon ground white pepper (or ground black pepper)
2 teaspoons Celtic sea salt

INSTRUCTIONS

1. In a medium bowl, beat eggs, 1 teaspoon salt and pepper until light and frothy, about 2 minutes. Sift almond flour into bowl and mix until dough comes together.
2. *Cover dough with parchment, if preferred, and refrigerate 2 - 4 hours.
3. Add 1 teaspoon salt to large pot of water and bring to boil. Add vegetable stock to medium pot and heat over medium heat.
4. Remove dough from refrigerator and roll into balls. Carefully place dough balls in boiling water. Reduce heat to low, cover and simmer 20 minutes, until cooked through.
5. Transfer matzo balls to serving dish with slotted spoon. Ladle heated vegetable stock over matzo balls and serve hot.

Butternut Squash Soup

Prep Time: 10 minutes
Cook Time: 1 hour
Servings: 4

INGREDIENTS

1 medium-large butternut squash (about 2 cups diced)
2 cups veggie stock
1/2 cup coconut milk (optional)
1/2 onion (white, yellow or sweet)
1/2 large carrot
1/2 celery stalk
1/2 teaspoon ground coriander (optional)
1 cinnamon stick
Ground black pepper, to taste
Celtic sea salt, to taste
2 tablespoons shelled pumpkin seeds (toasted or raw)
2 tablespoons ghee (or coconut oil)
2 tablespoons coconut oil

INSTRUCTIONS

1. Heat oven to 375 degrees F. Heat medium cast iron pan over medium-high heat. Add butter to hot oiled pan.
2. Peel squash and remove seeds. Dice and add to hot oiled pan with salt and pepper, to taste. Sauté until golden, about 3 - 4 minutes.

Place pan in oven and roast until browned on all sides, about 15 minutes.
3. Heat medium pot over medium-low heat. Add coconut oil to hot pot.
4. Peel and dice onion, celery and carrot. Add to hot oiled pot with cinnamon stick, salt and pepper to taste. Sauté until soft but not browned, about 10 minutes.
5. Remove squash from oven and let cool slightly. Add food processor or high-speed blender and process until puréed.
6. Add vegetable broth and coriander (optional) to pot. Increase heat to medium and bring to boil. Simmer about 5 minutes.
7. Stir in squash purée and simmer about 10 minutes. Discard cinnamon stick.
8. Add mixture to food processor or high-speed blender and purée until smooth. Or blend with immerse or stick blender until smooth.
9. Transfer mixture back to hot pot and stir in coconut milk (optional). Transfer to serving dish.
10. Sprinkle with pumpkin seeds and cracked black pepper. Serve hot.

Mexican Tomato Soup

Prep Time: 10 minutes

Cook Time: 40 minutes

Servings: 4

INGREDIENTS

2 cans (14.5 oz) organic crushed tomatoes

2 cans (11.5) organic tomato juice

5 large tomatoes (or 10 plum tomatoes)

1/2 cup coconut milk

1 red bell pepper (or 1/4 cup roasted red peppers, jarred)

1/4 red onion (or yellow or white onion)

2 garlic cloves

1/2 Serrano chili pepper (or other chili pepper) (optional)

1 tablespoon tapioca flour (or arrowroot powder)

2 tablespoons fresh Mexican oregano (or 1 teaspoon dried oregano)

2 large basil leaves

1 teaspoon fresh cracked black pepper (or ground black pepper)

Celtic sea salt, to taste

1 small bunch cilantro (for garnish)

2 tablespoons ghee (or cacao butter, or coconut oil)

INSTRUCTIONS

1. Juice tomatoes and set aside.

2. Roast red bell pepper over stove burner or until broiler, if using. Turn to char on all sides until skins sears. Rub off blackened skin. Cut in half and remove seeds, stem and veins.
3. Heat medium pot over medium-high heat. Add fat to hot pot.
4. Peel onion and garlic. Dice onion, roasted and red pepper. Mince garlic and Serrano pepper (optional). Add to hot oiled pot and sauté until fragrant, about 2 minutes.
5. Add tapioca and coconut milk. Stir to combine. Let cook about 2 minutes.
6. Chiffon (thinly slice) basil. Add to pot with tomato juice, crushed tomatoes, oregano, pepper and salt, to taste. Stir to combine.
7. Bring to simmer, then reduce heat to low. Simmer and reduce about 30 minutes, or until desired consistency is reached.
8. Transfer to serving dish. Chop cilantro and sprinkle over dish for garnish.
9. Serve hot.

Creamy "Cheesy" Broccoli Soup

Prep Time: 10 minutes

Cook Time: 30 minutes

Servings: 4

INGREDIENTS

1 large head broccoli

2 cups vegetable broth

1 cup nut milk

1/2 cup nutritional yeast

1 medium onion (white or yellow)

2 garlic cloves

1 tablespoon coconut aminos (or liquid aminos or tamari)

1 tablespoon mustard powder

Celtic sea salt, to taste.

1 teaspoon ground white pepper (or 1/2 teaspoon ground black pepper)

2 tablespoons bacon fat (or coconut oil, cacao butterr ghee)

Water

INSTRUCTIONS

1. Heat medium pot over medium heat. Add fat or oil to hot pot.
2. Peel onion and garlic. Chop and add to hot pot. Sauté until fragrant, about 2 minutes.
3. Chop broccoli and add to pot with vegetable broth. Increase heat and bring to boil. Cover and boil about 15 - 20 minutes until broccoli is softened.

4. Pour pot in to food processor or high-speed blender with nutritional yeast, coconut aminos, spices and salt, to taste. Process until smooth, about 1 - 2 minutes. Add enough water to reach desired consistency.
5. Transfer to serving dish and serve immediately.
6. Or add back to pot and heat through over medium heat. Then serve.

Pita Bites

Prep Time: *5 minutes

Cook Time: 20 minutes

Servings: 1

INGREDIENTS

Pita Bites

1 cup tapioca flour/starch

1 teaspoon ground chia seed (or flax meal)

1 egg

2 tablespoons coconut oil

1/4 cup water

1/2 teaspoon baking soda

1/4 teaspoon sea salt

Almond Hummus

1 cup skinless almonds

1/3 cup tahini

1 garlic clove

Juice of 1/2 lemon

Zest of 1/2 lemon

1/4 teaspoon sea salt

1/4 cup water

2 tablespoons pine nuts

INSTRUCTIONS

1. *Soak almonds overnight in enough water to cover. Drain and rinse.
2. Preheat oven to 375 degrees F. Cover sheet pan with parchment paper or baking mat. Heat small pot over low heat.
3. For *Pita Bites*, mix 1/3 cup tapioca flour with chia meal, water and 1 tablespoon coconut oil in pot. Stir until mixture comes together. Remove from heat and cool in freezer.
4. In medium bowl, blend remaining tapioca flour, baking soda and salt. Then add egg and remaining oil. Mix until combined.
5. Add cooled chia mixture to bowl and mix to combine. Then remove and knead to form dough.
6. Form large round disk, then use rolling pin to flatten on lined baking sheet. Cut out circles with biscuit cutter or drinking glass, or cut triangles with pizza cutter. Re-roll excess dough and repeat until all dough is used.
7. Arrange pita pieces on sheet pan and place in oven. Bake about 10 minutes. Carefully turn over with spatula and bake another 5 - 7 minutes, or until crisp.
8. Remove from oven and let cool completely. Place in lidded container or sealable lunch bag and serve room temperature.
9. For *Almond Hummus*, add 1/2 of water to all ingredients in food processor or bullet blender and process. Add just enough water to smooth blend.
10. Scrape hummus into lidded container and serve chilled or room temperature with *Pita Bites*.

Simple Gazpacho + Tortilla Chips

Prep Time: 20 minutes

Cook Time: 10 minutes

Servings: 4

INGREDIENTS

Grain-Free Tortillas

Gazpacho

2 (11.5 oz) cans organic tomato juice (or 3 cups juiced tomatoes)

4 plum tomatoes

2 red bell peppers

1 red onion

1 cucumber

3 garlic cloves

1/4 cup apple cider vinegar

1/4 cup coconut oil (or 2 tablespoons coconut oil and 2 tablespoons flavorful oil [walnut, almond, sesame, etc.])

1 teaspoon cracked black pepper (or ground black pepper)

1/2 tablespoon sea salt

INSTRUCTIONS

1. Seed cucumber and tomatoes. Seed, stem and vein bell peppers. Peel onion and garlic. Dice veggies, mince garlic, and add to medium serving bowl.

2. Add tomato juice, vinegar, oil, salt and pepper, and mix well. Place in refrigerator.
3. Heat medium pan over medium-high heat and coat with coconut oil.
4. For *Tortilla Chips*, prepare *Grain-Free Tortillas*.
5. Add more coconut oil to hot pan and allow to heat up. Cut tortillas into wedges with pizza cutter or sharp knife.
6. Add tortilla wedges back to hot pan in single layer and cook about 30 seconds on each side, until golden and crisp. Drain on paper towel. Repeat with remaining tortilla wedges.
7. Transfer warm *Tortilla Chips* to serving dish. Serve immediately with chilled *Gazpacho*.

Grain-Free Tortillas

Prep Time: 5 minutes
Cook Time: 10 minutes
Servings: 2

INGREDIENTS

2 tablespoons almond flour
2 tablespoons coconut flour
1/2 tablespoon flax meal (or ground chia seed)
2 eggs
1/4 cup water (plus extra)
2 tablespoons coconut oil
1/4 teaspoon baking powder
Coconut oil (for cooking)

INSTRUCTIONS

1. Heat medium frying pan over medium-high heat and coat with coconut oil.
2. Whisk together eggs, coconut oil and 1/4 cup water in medium bowl.
3. In separate mixing bowl, blend coconut flour, almond flour, flax or chia seed, and baking powder.
4. Slowly whisk as you pour flour mixture into wet ingredients. If batter appears too thick to spread fairly thin in pan, add up to 4 tablespoon water 1 tablespoon at a time.

5. Use ladle or dry measure cup to pour 1/2 of batter into hot oiled pan. Tilt pan in circular motion as you pour so batter spreads thinly.
6. Cook batter for about 2 minutes or until slightly golden and firm. Flip tortilla with tongs or spatula and cook another 2 minutes. Remove and place on paper towel or parchment.
7. Cook remaining batter for 2 minutes on each side. Re-oil pan as necessary.
8. Fill warm tortillas with meat or veggies of choice and serve warm.

Veggie Burger

Prep Time: 5 minutes

Cook Time: 20 minutes

Servings: 4

INGREDIENTS

Soft Burger Bun

Veggie Burger

2 eggs

1/2 head cauliflower

2 medium carrots

1 small white onion

1 cup walnuts (1/2 cup ground)

1/4 cup almond flour

2 tablespoons tapioca flour

2 tablespoons ground chia seed (or flax meal)

2 cloves garlic

1 teaspoon paprika

1 teaspoon ground black pepper

1 teaspoon sea salt

Topping

1 avocado

1 heirloom tomato

1 white onion

2 ribs romaine lettuce (or preferred lettuce)

INSTRUCTIONS
1. Preheat oven to 350 degrees F. Line sheet pan with parchment paper, or lightly coat with coconut oil. Or lightly coat 6 mini round cake pans with coconut oil.
2. Prepare *Soft Burger Buns* and place in oven.
3. While bread bakes, line dish with parchment paper.
4. Add walnuts and almond four to food processor or bullet blender. Process until finely ground. Add to medium mixing bowl.
5. Peel small onion and garlic. Add to processor or blender with cauliflower and carrots. Process until finely ground. Add eggs, tapioca and chia. Process until mixture becomes thickened and has batter-like consistency.
6. Add veggie mixture and spices to mixing bowl. Mix all ingredients together with hands or wooden spoon until fully combined and uniform.
7. Form veggie mixture into 4 patties and place on parchment lined dish. Place in freezer for 10 minutes.
8. Heat medium skillet over medium-high heat and add 1 tablespoon coconut oil.
9. Peel onion. Make 4 thick slices, keeping full ring intact. Using spatula, place full rings into hot oiled pan. Sear 1 minute on each side. Set aside on paper towel to drain.
10. Reduce heat to medium and coat pan with coconut oil.
11. Remove veggie patties from freezer and place in hot oiled pan. Cook 5 minutes, then carefully flip with spatula and cook another 5 minutes.

12. Remove *Soft Burger Bun* from oven and let cool about 5 minutes.
13. Cut lettuce ribs in half. Cut tomato into 4 thick slices. Slice avocado in half, pit and slice flesh in peel.
14. Slice bun in half and place lettuce on bottom bun, followed by tomato slice. Add burger patty, then grilled onion ring. Finish with a few slices of avocado and top bun.
15. Serve immediately.

Soft Burger Buns

Prep Time: 5 minutes
Cook Time: 15 minutes
Servings: 6

INGREDIENTS

1/4 cup almond flour
1/4 cup coconut flour
4 eggs
2 tablespoons coconut oil
2 tablespoons unsweetened applesauce
1 teaspoon flax meal (or ground chia seed)
1 teaspoon baking powder
1/2 teaspoon sea salt

INSTRUCTIONS

1. Preheat oven to 350 degrees F. Line sheet pan with parchment paper, or lightly coat with coconut oil. Or lightly coat 6 mini round cake pans with coconut oil.
2. Beat eggs, coconut oil and applesauce in medium mixing bowl with hand mixer or whisk.
3. In large mixing bowl, sift together coconut flour, almond flour, flax or chia meal, baking powder and salt. Pour egg mixture into flour mixture and mix until combined.

4. Scoop thick batter onto prepared sheet pan in six 4 inch rounds. Or pour into six prepared mini cake pans for uniformity. Smooth batter with knife or spatula.
5. Place in oven and bake for 12 - 15 minutes, or until tops are firm to the touch and golden.
6. Remove from oven and let cool at least 5 minutes.
7. Slice in half and serve with your favorite patty or filling.

Egg Salad Sandwich

Prep Time: 5 minutes

Cook Time: 15 minutes

Servings: 2

INGREDIENTS

Sandwich Bread

Avocado Egg Salad

8 eggs

1 avocado

1/4 cup dill pickle relish

3 tablespoons organic mustard

2 teaspoons paprika

1/2 teaspoon ground black pepper

1/4 teaspoon sea salt

INSTRUCTIONS

1. Preheat oven to 350 degrees F. Lightly coat 6 mini round cake pans or medium loaf pan with coconut oil. Bring medium pot of lightly salted water to a boil.
2. Prepare *Sandwich Bread* and place in oven.
3. While bread bakes, gently add eggs to hot water with tongs and cook about 8 - 10 minutes.
4. Drain eggs in colander and run under cold water to cool.

5. While eggs cool, slice and pit avocado. Scoop flesh into medium mixing bowl. Add relish, mustard, salt and spices.
6. Crack eggs shells and peel. Add boiled eggs to medium mixing bowl.
7. Using a fork, mash ingredients together until smooth mixture with soft chunks forms.
8. Remove *Sandwich Bread* from oven and let cool about 5 minutes.
9. Slice bread and fill with *Avocado Egg Salad*.
10. Serve immediately. Or refrigerate about 20 minutes and serve chilled.

Sandwich Bread

Prep Time: 5 minutes

Cook Time: 15 minutes

Servings: 6

INGREDIENTS

2 cups almond flour

4 eggs

1/2 cup coconut cream (or melted cacao butter)

1/2 cup arrowroot powder (or tapioca flour)

1/3 cup ground chia seed (or flax meal)

1/4 cup coconut oil

2 tablespoons unsweetened applesauce

1 teaspoon apple cider vinegar

1 teaspoon baking soda

1/2 teaspoon sea salt

INSTRUCTIONS

1. Preheat oven to 350 degrees F. Lightly coat 6 mini round cake pans with coconut oil.
2. Beat eggs, coconut oil, coconut cream, applesauce and vinegar in medium mixing bowl with hand mixer or whisk.
3. In large mixing bowl, sift together almond flour, arrowroot, chia meal, baking soda and salt. Pour egg mixture into flour mixture and mix until well combined.

4. Pour batter into prepared mini cake pans and bake for about 15 minutes, or until golden brown and toothpick inserted comes out clean.
5. Remove from oven and let cool at least 5 minutes.
6. Slice in half and serve with your favorite deli meats or sandwich salads.

NOTE: Lightly oil medium loaf pan and bake for about 25 minutes for **Sandwich Bread** loaf.

Kelp Noodle Salad

Prep Time: 5 minutes
Cook Time: 5 minutes
Servings: 2

INGREDIENTS

1 package (12 oz) kelp noodles
1/2 lemon
1 small cucumber
1 small red bell pepper
1 large carrot
Small bunch cilantro
2 large basil leaves

Orange Avocado Dressing
1 avocado
1 large orange
1/2 lemon
5 large basil leaves
1/4 teaspoon ground black pepper
1/4 teaspoon cayenne pepper or red pepper flake (optional)
Large bunch cilantro

INSTRUCTIONS

1. Rinse and drain kelp noodles. Add to medium bowl and soak 5 minutes in warm water and juice of 1/2 lemon. Or bring medium

pot of water with juice of 1/2 lemon to a boil and cook kelp noodles for 5 minutes, if softer texture preferred.
2. Peel, seed and cut cucumber in half width-wise. Cut bell pepper in half, then remove stem, seeds and veins. Use vegetable peeler or grater to make long, thin slices of carrot. Thinly slice cucumber and bell pepper lengthwise.
3. Add veggies and drained kelp noodles to medium mixing bowl.
4. For *Orange Avocado Dressing*, add basil and cilantro leaves to food processor or bullet blender with juice of orange and process to break down leaves. Slice avocado in half and remove pit. Scoop flesh into processor with juice of 1/2 lemon, black pepper and hot pepper (optional). Process until thick and until creamy.
5. Pour *Orange Avocado Dressing* over sliced veggies and kelp noodles. Toss to coat.
6. Serve immediately. Or refrigerate for 20 minutes and serve chilled.

Zucchini Salad with Sundried Tomato Sauce

Prep Time: 20 minutes*

Servings: 2

INGREDIENTS

1 medium zucchini

1 tomato

5 sundried tomatoes

1 garlic clove

2 fresh basil leaves

1 tablespoon raw virgin coconut oil (or 2 tablespoons warm water)

1/4 teaspoon ground white pepper (or black pepper)

1/4 teaspoon sea salt

INSTRUCTIONS

1. Run zucchini through spiralizer, slice into long, thin shreds with knife, or use vegetable peeler to make flat, thin slices. Sprinkle with a pinch of salt and pepper, and gently toss to coat.
2. Add tomato, sundried tomatoes, peeled garlic, basil, coconut oil or warm water, and remaining salt and pepper to food processor or bullet blender. Process until sauce of desired consistency forms.
3. Transfer zucchini pasta to serving bowls. Top with tomato sauce and serve immediately.
4. Or refrigerate for 20 minutes and serve chilled.

Quick Raw Avocado Slaw

Prep Time: 10 minutes*

Cook Time: 20 minutes

Servings: 4

INGREDIENTS

1/2 head cabbage (2 cups shredded)

1 avocado

1 carrot

Zest of 1 lemon

Juice of 1 lemon

1 tablespoon raw honey

2 tablespoons apple cider vinegar

1 teaspoon ground white pepper (or black pepper)

1 teaspoon sea salt

INSTRUCTIONS

1. Cut avocado in half and remove pit. Scoop flesh into large mixing bowl and mash with fork.
2. Remove any tough outer leaves and core from cabbage. Shred cabbage and carrot. Add to bowl with vinegar, honey, salt and pepper. Zest *then* juice lemon, and add.
3. Toss to combine.
4. Serve immediately. Or and place in refrigerator for 20 minutes and serve chilled.

Vegetarian Texas Chili

Prep Time: 10 minutes*

Servings: 2

INGREDIENTS

5 - 6 plum tomatoes

1/2 teaspoon dried cumin

1/4 teaspoon chili powder

1/4 teaspoon onion powder

1/4 teaspoon garlic powder

1 teaspoon fresh oregano leaves (or 1/4 teaspoon dried oregano)

1/2 teaspoon ground black pepper

1/4 teaspoon cayenne pepper or red pepper flakes (optional)

1 teaspoon Celtic sea salt

1 teaspoon chia seed (or flax seed)

1/2 cup raw cashews

Water

INSTRUCTIONS

1. *Soak raw cashews in enough water to cover overnight in refrigerator. Drain and rinse. Set aside.
2. Grind chia or flax in food processor or high-speed blender. Set aside.
3. Juice tomatoes. Or add to food processor or high-speed blender and process. Add enough water to reach desired consistency, if necessary. Then strain.

4. Add tomato juice, ground chia or flax, 1/2 of soaked cashews, salt, pepper and spices to blender. Process until smooth, about 1 - 2 minutes.
5. Stir in remaining soaked cashews.
6. Pour into serving bowls and serve immediately.

Caesar Salad

Prep Time: 10 minutes

Servings: 1

INGREDIENTS

2 cups chopped romaine lettuce

Almond Parmesan

1/4 cup raw almonds

1 teaspoon raw apple cider vinegar

1 teaspoon nutritional yeast (optional)

1/4 teaspoon garlic powder

1/4 teaspoon onion powder

1/4 teaspoon dried oregano

1/4 teaspoon Celtic sea salt

Caesar Dressing

2 tablespoons raw cashews (or raw sunflower seeds)

2 tablespoons raw sunflower seeds

1 tablespoon raw pine nuts (or raw sesame seeds or raw tahini)

2 tablespoons lemon juice

1 teaspoon sweetener*

1 garlic clove

3/4 teaspoon coconut aminos (or nutritional yeast)

1/2 teaspoon dried dill (optional)

Cracked or ground black pepper, to taste

Water

INSTRUCTIONS

1. Rinse, dry and plate romaine lettuce.
2. For *Almond Parmesan*, add almonds, vinegar, salt, spices and nutritional yeast (optional) to food processor or high-speed blender. Process until almonds are coarsely ground and resemble ground parmesan cheese. Set aside.
3. For *Caesar Dressing*, peel garlic and add to food processor or high-speed blender with sweetener and lemon juice. Process until smooth. Then add remaining ingredients and process until smooth, about 1 - 2 minutes. Add enough water to reach desired consistency.
4. Drizzle *Caesar Dressing* over salad and sprinkle with *Almond Parmesan*. Serve immediately.

raw honey or dried dates

Spiced Walnut Autumn Salad

Prep Time: 10 minutes

Servings: 1

INGREDIENTS

Salad

2 cups red lettuce leaves (or other colorful lettuce variety)

1/2 cup arugula

1/2 ripe pear

Spiced Walnuts

1/4 cup walnuts (halves or pieces)

1 tablespoons raw honey (or 1 dried date plus 1 tablespoon water)

1/4 teaspoon ground cinnamon

1/8 teaspoon ground ginger

1/4 teaspoon fresh ground nutmeg

1/8 teaspoon vanilla

1/4 teaspoon ground cardamom (optional)

Orange Vinaigrette

1 orange

2 tablespoons raw apple cider vinegar

2 teaspoons sweetener*

1 teaspoon raw walnut oil (or coconut, almond, sesame oil, etc.)

1 teaspoon raw tahini or sesame seeds (optional)

1 teaspoon ground mustard seeds (or whole mustard seeds)

1/4 teaspoon cracked or ground black pepper

INSTRUCTIONS

1. For *Salad*, rinse, dry and plate lettuce and arugula. Slice pear in half, and remove seeds. Top greens with sliced pears.
2. For *Spiced Walnuts*, process date and water in food processor or high-speed blender until smooth and add to small mixing bowl, if using. Or combine walnuts, spices and raw honey in small mixing bowl. Sprinkle over *Salad*.
3. For *Orange Vinaigrette*, zest and juice orange. Add to food processor or high-speed blender with vinegar, sweetener, spices and tahini (optional) and process until smooth, about 1 minute.
4. Drizzle *Orange Vinaigrette* over salad and serve immediately.

stevia, raw honey or dried dates

Pecan Apricot Spinach Salad

Prep Time: 10 minutes

Servings: 1

INGREDIENTS

Salad

2 cups spinach leaves

1/2 cup chopped kale leaves

4 - 5 dried apricots

3 tablespoons pecans (halves or pieces)

Honey Mustard Vinaigrette

2 tablespoons raw honey (or 2 dried dates + 2 tablespoons water)

2 tablespoons ground mustard (or mustard seed)

2 tablespoons raw apple cider vinegar

3 tablespoons raw oil (coconut, walnut, almond, sesame, etc.)

3/4 teaspoons Celtic sea salt

INSTRUCTIONS

1. For *Salad*, rinse, dry and plate spinach and kale. Chop dried apricots. Sprinkle apricots and pecans over greens.
2. For *Honey Mustard Vinaigrette*, add honey, mustard, vinegar, oil and salt to food processor or high-speed blender and process until smooth, about 1 minute.
3. Drizzle *Honey Mustard Vinaigrette* over salad and serve immediately.

Southern Style Egg Salad

Prep Time: 5 minutes

Cook Time: 15 minutes

Servings: 4

INGREDIENTS

8 cage-free eggs

1 avocado

1 celery stalk

1/4 sweet onion

1/4 cup sweet pickle relish (or dill pickle relish + 1 tablespoon raw honey, agave or date butter)

1/4 cup organic mustard

2 teaspoons paprika

1/2 teaspoon ground black pepper

1/4 teaspoon Celtic sea salt

INSTRUCTIONS
1. Bring medium pot of lightly salted water to a boil. Leave enough room in pot for eggs.
2. Gently add eggs to hot water with tongs and cook about 10 minutes.
3. Drain eggs into colander in sink. Fill pot with cold water and add eggs back to pot. Let cold water run slowly over eggs in pot to cool.

4. Slice and pit avocado. Scoop flesh into medium mixing bowl. Thinly slice celery. Peel and finely dice onion. Add to mixing bowl with relish, mustard, salt and spices. Mix with large spoon to combine.
5. Crack cooled eggs and peel off shells. Add boiled eggs to medium mixing bowl.
6. Use a fork or knife to chop eggs. Use large spoon to mix and mash ingredients together until smooth mixture with soft chunks forms. Stir to combine.
7. Transfer to serving dish and serve immediately. Or refrigerate about 20 minutes and serve chilled.

Pesto Tomato Caprese

Prep Time: 5 minutes

Servings: 2

INGREDIENTS

1 large yellow tomato

1 large red tomato

Small bunch fresh basil

Celtic sea salt, to taste

Crack or ground black pepper, to taste

Basil Pesto

2 cups basil leaves (packed)

1/4 cup raw pine nuts

1/2 - 1/3 cup raw oil (coconut, walnut, almond, sesame, etc.)

2 garlic cloves

1/2 lemon (or 1 tablespoon raw apple cider vinegar)

1/4 teaspoon Celtic sea salt

INSTRUCTIONS

1. For *Basil Pesto*, peel garlic and add to food processor or high-speed blender with squeeze of 1/2 lemon. Process until finely chopped. Add pine nuts, basil, oil and salt and process until finely ground, about 1 minute.
2. Slice tomatoes and plate in alternating colors. Sprinkle with salt and pepper. Chiffon basil leaves.

3. Spread *Basil Pesto* over tomato slices and top with fresh basil. Serve immediately.

Cashew Crunch Kelp Noodle Salad

Prep Time: 10 minutes*

Servings: 2

INGREDIENTS

1 package (12 oz) kelp noodles

1/2 lemon

1/2 small red bell pepper

Cashew Sauce

1 cup raw cashews

1/2 small red bell pepper

1/2 lemon

1 tablespoon coconut aminos (or raw apple cider vinegar)

2 large basil leaves

1/2 teaspoon smoked paprika

1/2 teaspoon ground black pepper

1/2 teaspoon Celtic sea salt

1/4 teaspoon ground turmeric (optional)

1/4 teaspoon smoked chili powder (optional)

Water

INSTRUCTIONS

1. *Soak 3/4 cup cashews in enough water to cover at least 4 hours, or overnight in refrigerator. Drain and rinse.

2. Drain and rinse kelp noodles. Add to medium bowl with warm water and juice of 1/2 lemon. Set aside 5 minutes.

3. Cut bell pepper in half. Remove stem, seeds and veins and set half of pepper aside. Julienne (thinly slice) remaining bell pepper and add to medium mixing bowl.

4. For *Crunchy Cashew Sauce*, add soaked cashews, bell pepper, juice of 1/2 lemon, coconut aminos, basil, salt and spices to food processor or high-speed blender. Process until smooth, about 2 minutes. Add enough water to reach desired consistency. Set aside.

5. Drain kelp noodles and add to sliced bell pepper. Add *Cashew Sauce* and toss to coat. Transfer noodles to serving dishes.

6. Roughly chop remaining 1/4 cup cashews. Sprinkle noodles and serve immediately. Or refrigerate for 20 minutes and serve chilled.

Dill Stuffed Tomatoes

Prep Time: 15 minutes*

Servings: 2

INGREDIENTS

4 medium tomatoes

1 celery stalk

1 small carrot

1 green onion (scallion)

1/3 cup sunflower seeds

1/2 red bell pepper

1/4 small red onion (or sweet onion)

1/2 teaspoon Celtic sea salt

Dill Dressing

1/2 cup raw cashews

1 tablespoon raw apple cider vinegar (or coconut aminos)

1 teaspoon ground mustard (or mustard seeds)

1/2 lemon

1 small garlic clove

2 sprigs fresh dill

1/2 teaspoon Celtic sea salt

1/4 teaspoon ground white pepper (or pinch ground black pepper)

Water

INSTRUCTIONS

1. *Soak cashews in enough water to cover at least 4 hours, or overnight in refrigerator. Drain and rinse.
2. Cut tops off tomatoes and scoop out seeds. Set aside.
3. Finely dice celery and carrot. Slice green onion. Peel and dice onion. Add to medium mixing bowl. Remove stem, seeds and veins from bell pepper, then dice. Add to bowl with sprinkle of salt. Set aside.
4. For *Dill Dressing*, peel garlic and add to food processor or high-speed blender with soaked cashews, vinegar, mustard, squeeze of lemon, dill, salt and pepper. Process until smooth and creamy, about 1 - 2 minutes. Add enough water to reach desired consistency.
5. Pour *Dill Dressing* over chopped veggies. Toss to coat.
6. Plate hollowed tomatoes and stuff with *Dill Dressing* veggie mixture. Serve immediately.

Squash Blossom Stuffers

Prep Time: 10 minutes*

Servings: 4

INGREDIENTS

16 squash blossoms

1/2 cup walnuts

1 avocado

1 small onion

1/2 sprig fresh dill

1/2 lemon

1/2 teaspoon dried thyme

1/2 teaspoon ground white pepper (or ground black pepper)

1/2 teaspoon Celtic sea salt

1 teaspoon dried tarragon (optional)

Water

INSTRUCTIONS
1. *Gently rinse blossoms and pat dry. Let air dry for 30 minutes.
2. Cut avocado in half and remove pit. Scoop flesh into food processor or high-speed blender with walnuts, dill, squeeze of lemon, salt, pepper and spices. Process until smooth, about 2 minutes. Add enough water to reach desired consistency.
3. Peel onion and mince. Add to small mixing bowl with avocado mixture. Mix to combine.
4. Spoon mixture into squash blossoms. Serve immediately.

Indian Egg Fried Rice

Prep Time: 10 minutes

Cook Time: 15 minutes

Servings: 2

INGREDIENTS

1/2 head cauliflower

4 cage-free eggs

1 small carrot

1/2 red bell pepper

1/2 yellow bell pepper

1/4 onion (yellow or white)

2 small green onions (scallions)

2 tablespoons pure fish sauce (or coconut aminos or liquid aminos)

1 tablespoon coconut aminos (or coconut vinegar or liquid aminos)

1 teaspoon raw honey (or date butter or agave)

1 teaspoon sesame oil (optional)

1 large garlic clove

1/2 piece fresh ginger

1/2 teaspoon red pepper flake

Celtic sea salt, to taste

Coconut oil (for cooking)

Water

INSTRUCTIONS

1. Cut cauliflower into florets and add to food processor with shredding attachment to rice. Or finely mince cauliflower. Set aside.
2. Heat medium pan or wok over high heat. Lightly coat with coconut oil.
3. Whisk eggs in medium mixing bowl. Set aside.
4. Remove stems, seeds and veins from bell peppers, then julienne (thinly slice). Finely dice carrot. Slice green onions. Peel and mince garlic, ginger and onion.
5. Add red pepper flakes to hot oiled pan. Sauté until just cooked fragrant, about 30 seconds. Add garlic, ginger and onion and sauté about 1 minute.
6. Add cauliflower to hot pan. Sauté about 5 minutes, until cauliflower is golden and a bit softened.
7. Add carrot, peppers and 1/2 green onions. Cook another 2 - 5 minutes, until cauliflower is cooked through. Add a few tablespoons of water and cover with lid to steam, if desired.
8. Push veggies aside and make well (opening) in center of pan. Pour whisked eggs into well in center and carefully scramble until fully cooked, about 2 minutes. Mix eggs into veggies.
9. Remove from heat and transfer to serving dish. Sprinkle remaining green onions over dish and serve hot.